Markets of New England

Markets of New England

Christine Chitnis

THE LITTLE BOOKROOM
New York

Library of Congress Cataloging-in-Publication Data

Chitnis, Christine.
Markets of New England / by Christine Chitnis ;
photographs by Christine Chitnis.
p. cm.
Includes index.
ISBN 1-892145-96-0 (alk. paper)
1. Farmers' markets--New England--Guidebooks. 2. Craft festivals--
New England--Guidebooks. I. Title.
HF5472.U7N33 2011
381'.410974--dc22
2010046407

Published by The Little Bookroom
435 Hudson Street, Suite 300
New York NY 10014
editorial@littlebookroom.com
www.littlebookroom.com

10 9 8 7 6 5 4 3 2 1

To my boys. . . who came along for the ride.

To Mom and Dad. . . for everything.

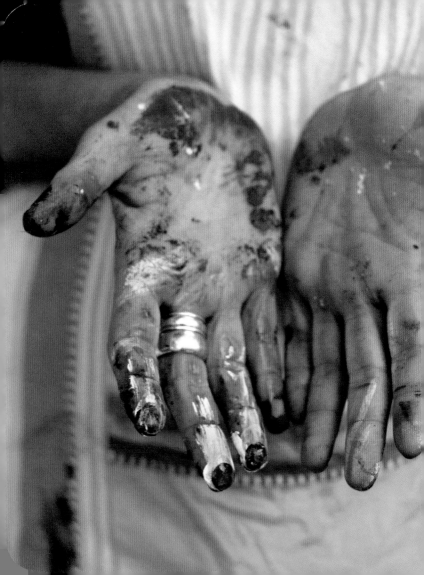

Markets
of New
England

Christine Chitnis

Lilac RiDGE

r Own
esh Picked
Sweet
Onions
3.50

Contents

Introduction

When we use our collective consumer power to support artisans—beekeepers, cheese mongers, weavers, and woodworkers—we are insuring that our communities remain unique, thriving places to live. In this age of big-box stores and mass-produced items, it has become all the more important to invest in our local economy. . . one artist, one farmer, one shop at a time.

My passion for supporting local artisans leads back to my childhood, which was idyllic. My mom left her career in nursing to stay home with me and my brothers, and many of my lifelong passions were formed during the years I spent by her side, planting gardens in our sloping yard, sewing tiny quilts for my dolls, and visiting the food co-op to stock up on bulk granola. It is obvious to me now that my mom was ahead of her time—she was a believer in an organic, homemade lifestyle.

People across the country are discovering the immense pleasure that can be had by living a simple, pared-down life full of farm-fresh food and handmade possessions, generating an increasing interest in buying locally grown and produced goods. There are no better places to "shop local" than at neighborhood farmers' markets and art events.

We are often encouraged to "buy local," and indeed, that is the focus of this book, but what exactly does that mean, and why is it so important? Buying products at locally owned businesses and from local farmers and artists keeps that money circulating closer to home. There is a direct link between healthy communities and healthy local economies. According to the 3/50 Project, "For every $100 spent in locally owned independent stores, $68 returns to the community through taxes, payroll, and other expenditures. If you spend that in a national chain, only $43 stays local. Spend it online and nothing comes home."

When you shop locally, also, you ensure the diversity of our Main Streets and you help to maintain community character and individuality. Additionally, artists and farmers, when properly supported by their community, can then keep alive age-old traditions of their crafts and skills.

In keeping with this line of thinking, when choosing which markets to feature in this book, I decided that events had to be situated near a town (as opposed to a stand-alone convention center off the highway), had to be operated by a local organization, and had to fairly benefit the farmers and craftspeople selling their wares.

I have included a wide range of events in this book, stretching the concept of "markets" to its limit along the way. When it comes to art events, you will find everything from funky, indie art markets, such as the Queen City Craft Bazaar in Burlington, to more traditional art festivals, such as the Berkshires Art Festival in Massachusetts. I have also included several open studio tours, such as the Vermont Crafts Council Open Studio Weekend.

While it's a bit harder to veer "off track" when it comes to farmers' markets, I have managed to throw in a few surprises, such as a one-of-a-kind, floating farmers' market and a community-enriching plant sale.

It is my hope that by including such a diverse selection of

events, there will be something that appeals to everyone.

What to Expect

It is very rare to find a store where every item for sale appeals to your taste, and the same goes for market shopping. Though I have tried to include worthwhile markets that have something to offer everyone, it can often be hit-or-miss, especially at art and craft events. I usually find that for every twenty booths, there might be one or two that really grab my attention, and usually only the work of a handful of artists leaves a lasting impression. This process of sifting and sorting through the offerings is simply part of the experience when it comes to market shopping.

Supporting Our Artisans

In an effort to credit all of the talented artists and farmers featured throughout the book, I have listed them in the Featured Artisans section by name, website, and the page number on which they, or their work, appear. If you see something that catches your eye, please pay a visit to their website and use your consumer power to support their handmade, homemade products.

More Market Offerings

While this is not a complete guide to every artisan market in New England, it is my best attempt at highlighting the most vibrant, unique, and thriving events. I encourage you to check out the additional resources listed in the back of the book to come up with a market itinerary of your very own.

Also keep in mind that markets are always evolving. Hours, locations, and times of year can change and some markets may close for good. Please visit each market's website for the most up-to-date information before you plan your trip.

Maine

Farmers' Markets

Craft Markets

Belfast Farmers' Market

Front Street, Belfast
(Main Street on select Fridays)
Friday 9am–1pm, May–October
www.belfastfarmersmarket.org

The picture-perfect coastal town of Belfast on Penobscot Bay has long been a center for various types of commerce: a summer fishing ground for the Abenaki Indians in the seventeenth century, a trading post and town settled by Scotch/Irish immigrants in the eighteenth, and a prosperous shipbuilding center in the late nineteenth, turning lumber from the Maine woods brought down the Passagassawakeag River from Bangor, into five-masted schooners. You can visit mansions built by the wealthy shipbuilders around this small town in several architectural styles: Greek Revival, Italianate, and Federal.

Today, commerce is thriving at the Belfast Farmers' Market, which has grown immensely in the past few years. In addition to the plentiful offerings of produce, you may find blueberry tea, pastries, fresh seafood, homemade preserves, grass-fed beef and lamb, raspberry lemonade, handwoven baskets, and yarn. On select Fridays, the market moves from the harbor to Main Street, where it is held in conjunction with the monthly Main Street Festival, complete with musical entertainment, dancing, jugglers, face painting, and artist demonstrations. A winter market is held over several Fridays in November and December.

Portland Farmers' Market

Monument Square, Portland
Monday and Wednesday 7am–2pm

Deering Oaks Park, Portland
Saturday 7am–12pm
April–November

www.portlandmainefarmersmarket.org

Winter Farmers Market
Saturday 9am–1pm, January–April
(see website for location)
www.portlandmainewintermarket.com

Portland's farmers' market dates back to 1768, which means the city has been celebrating farm-fresh goodness for more than two centuries. It is often voted one of the top farmers' markets in the country, and after paying a visit to the Saturday event, it isn't hard to see why. At the peak of sunflower season, the cheery bouquets of flowers that spill out from almost every booth seem to encapsulate the sunny attitude of this well-attended market.

Over thirty vendors line the shaded walkways of Deering Oaks Park on Saturday, all offering Maine-grown produce and products. Foodies will especially appreciate hard-to-find delicacies such as homemade tempeh from Lalibela Farm; red-cabbage sauerkraut and kimchi from Thirty-Acre Farm; black radishes, raw honey, and kefir from Swallowtail Farm; and, of course, plenty of freshly picked Maine blueberries.

Rockland Farmers' Market

Harbor Park, Rockland
Thursday 9am–12:30pm, May–October
www.rocklandfarmersmarket.org

T he picturesque port of Rockland has received all kinds of designations from different organizations over the years for different reasons: a top adventure town from the National Geographic Society, a Distinctive Destination from the National Historic Preservation Trust, and the Number 2 Cool Small Town in America from *Budget Travel*.

It's hard not to love a city that boasts three independent bookstores on a Main Street that measures less than a mile long. Rockland is a town that clearly loves its local businesses, a sentiment echoed at the weekly farmers' market held at Harbor Park. With an active harbor nearby, there is an abundance of freshly caught seafood, from pollack, monkfish and dab fillets to cleaned squid, whole lobster and snow crabmeat. The market also serves as a pick-up point for members of Port Clyde Fresh Catch's community-supported fisheries (CSF) program, which supplies its members with weekly shares of wild-caught Maine seafood from the Midcoast Fishermen's Cooperative.

Other tempting delicacies include Appleton Creamery's assorted artisanal cheeses. The crowd favorite, chevre marinated in olive oil with roasted garlic, peppercorns, bay leaf, and herbs, is perfect paired with a loaf of hearty, crusty bread from Atlantic Bakery. Aunt Polly's Pickles and Jams offers a wide selection of canned goods, including rarities such as pickled fiddle-heads. Maine-ly Poultry offers the usual chicken, eggs, and turkey, as well as rabbit, a rare farmers' market find. Finally, to satisfy your sweet tooth, look for Black Dinah Chocolatiers' handcrafted chocolates, made with fair-trade chocolate and local ingredients, and Stone Fox Farm Creamery's rich, creamy, all-natural handmade ice cream.

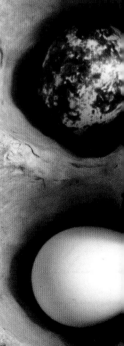

Merrymeeting Farm Market Boat

Southport Island
Friday, July–August (weather permitting)
11am Pratt's Island dock
12pm Town Landing at Newagen
2pm Capitol Island

David Berry is the captain of a 34-foot New Haven sharpie, the Beth Alison, which every Friday he stocks to the gills with organic produce from his farm in Bowdoinham, Maine. He then sails to various locations on Southport Island, where locals often gather on the docks to await his arrival. When the "veggie boat," as it's called, sails into port, David snaps open the boat's canvas awnings and rings the old brass school bell to signal he's open for business. Besides the abundant offerings of produce and cut flowers, Berry's wife Alison makes jams, chutneys, and pickles, as well as a variety of freshly baked goods. Rosemont Market, located in Portland, supplies David with cheese and a small variety of prepared foods. A typical day's offerings may include garlic scapes, wild blueberries, candy-striped beets, baby squash, blackberries, basil, sugar snap peas, garlic and herb goat cheese, pesto, a few jars of rhubarb jam, and a pan of freshly baked sticky buns.

Yarmouth Clam Festival

Main Street, Yarmouth

Friday–Sunday of the third weekend in July

www.clamfestival.com

The Yarmouth Clam Festival is something of a Maine institution, having been around for more than four decades. If you've ever wondered how many different ways you can cook a clam, then a visit to this event is a must. You'll find clams—fried, baked, stuffed, and chowdered—as well as a host of other goodies including lobster rolls, jumbo shrimp, fried dough, home-made cornbread, onion rings, fresh lemonade, and ice cream sandwiches.

Besides the good eats, there are activities galore, including a carnival, a parade, horse-and-buggy rides, musical guests, and, of course, a crafts market. While many of the items have a decidedly kitschy feel, there are a few outstanding crafters that make this a worthwhile market. Leather journals, fabric goods, and organic soaps are a few of the offerings. Whether or not you visit the craft section of the festivities, the Yarmouth Clam Festival is a not-to-be-missed event that celebrates summer on the coast.

SOAPS

Picnic Music and Arts Festival

Lincoln Park on Congress Street and Franklin Arterial, Portland
Saturday 11am–6pm in late August

Picnic Holiday Sale
Maine Irish Heritage Center, 34 Gray Street, Portland
Saturday–Sunday in early December

www.picnicportland.com

Over 100 carefully-selected vendors, selling everything from clothing and jewelry to photography and stationery, set up shop during the summertime Picnic Music and Arts Festival in Lincoln Park. Standouts include Alisha Gould Design's bright, graphic posters and prints, Shara Porter's edgy leather wallets and coin purses, Patti Sandberg's rustic nature-inspired pottery, Erin Flett's cheeky squirrel pillows, and the handmade toys from Finns and Flowers Toy Company. Healthy, delicious food, live music, and book signings round out the event. The same atmosphere is echoed at the Holiday Sale, although the festivities are moved indoors to the Maine Irish Heritage Center.

Cott

Ginger Ale

15 delicious flavors

Common Ground Country Fair

Common Ground Country Fairground, Unity
Friday–Sunday in late September, gates open at 9am
(see website for daily schedule)
Admission: $10, free for MOFGA members, kids 12 and under free
www.mofga.org

Every fall an estimated 60,000 visitors converge on the small town of Unity to partake in the festivities of the Common Ground Country Fair. Touted as a three-day celebration of Maine's rich rural and agricultural history, the fair boasts a packed roster of activities, including music, exhibits, sales, and demonstrations, all of which emphasize environmental sustainability, traditional craftsmanship, and organic farming. Formed in 1971, the Maine Organic Farmers and Gardeners Association (MOFGA), the oldest and largest state organic organization in the country, began hosting the fair over thirty years ago, and it has grown steadily since then.

Included on the extensive fairgrounds is the state's only all-organic farmers' market, a large agricultural pavilion where Maine farmers show their working animals, and a craft area, featuring only craftspeople who reside in Maine. The wares for sale at the fair run the gamut from hand-built chicken coops, starter beehives, worm bins, and gardening tools to kids' clothing, beeswax candles, books by Maine authors, furniture, and fine art photography. Saturday is the busiest of the three days, so consider visiting on Friday or Sunday.

At the food court, more than sixty food vendors serve Maine

grown and raised organic foods including wood-fired pizza, barbequed chicken and pork, tofu scrambles, lamb and falafel gyros, fruit smoothies, salads, stir fries, baked goods, homemade ice cream, lobster rolls, hand-cut French fries, and curries. Those looking for vegetarian, vegan, and gluten-free options have plenty to choose from. More than 700 workshops, presentations, and demonstrations are held over the course of the three days, covering everything from organic gardening and agriculture to cooking, energy-efficient building, and environmental, health, and social issues.

It's worth noting that with so many visitors flocking to the fair, the small country roads surrounding the fairground quickly become a traffic nightmare. Avoid the long lines and crowded parking lots by visiting MOFGA's website to find carpools in your area; alternatively, park at any of the park-and-ride lots and ride your bike the rest of the way (bikers save $2 on the ticket price). Another option is to take the Brooks Preservation Society train directly to the fairgrounds from stations in Unity and Thorndike (an all-day train pass costs $10 for adults and $5 for children ages 10 and under).

DANICA
CANDLEWORKS
HAND-DIPPED CANDLES
Rockport, ME 04856-0305

and
Birch Root beer
$3.00 bottle
$2.00
cup

The Maine Crafts Guild Shows

Various shows throughout Maine

www.mainecraftsguild.com for dates and locations

The Maine Crafts Guild is dedicated to preserving the rich heritage of the state's craftspeople through outreach programs, educational opportunities, and craft shows. Beginning in early July and ending in early November, the guild hosts one to two shows each month, spanning the state from Scarborough to Bar Harbor. Each show highlights the work of Maine's finest craftspeople and their commitment to preserving the traditions of their chosen craft, be it basket weaving, glassblowing, pottery, jewelry making, painting, woodworking, or fiber arts. The number of vendors on hand depends on the size of the venue, ranging from eighty artists at the Mount Desert Island show in Bar Harbor, to thirty at the Augusta show, held at the Maine State Museum.

The quality of work at The Maine Crafts Guild shows is always top of the line, as the artisans in attendance are often nationally recognized in their chosen fields. Pay a visit to the Craft Guilds website for a directory of their artists, most of whom welcome requests for studio visits, which can be a great alternative if your travel plans don't dovetail with one of the shows.

New Hampshire

Farmers' Markets

Craft Markets

Portsmouth Farmers' Market

City Hall, 1 Junkins Ave, Portsmouth
Saturday 8am–1pm, May–November
www.seacoastgrowers.org

Summer tourists looking for a quintessential New England getaway will find Portsmouth the ideal destination. Along with the town's trendy shops, picturesque harbors, and many restaurants, they'll find weekly farmers' markets offering an impressive array of produce, meats, dairy, and prepared foods. The artisanal goods available—from adorable hand-knit baby socks to boldly colored pottery—rival the quality found at most craft fairs. Erin Moran, a Portsmouth local, sells brightly hued pottery at many of the Saturday markets. Touching Earth Farm offers potted plants and artfully arranged succulent container plantings. The Jenness Farm stand displays goat milk soaps and a wide array of skin care products, as well as lavender laundry sachets. Above all, don't miss Toni's Donuts for freshly baked donuts to go with your morning coffee.

Newport Farmers' Market

North Main Street on the Town Common, Newport
Friday 3pm–6pm, June–October
www.newportnhmarket.org

Newport boasts New Hampshire's largest Town Common, which is put to good use every week hosting the Lake Sunapee region's largest farmers' market. Before the invention of the automobile, the eight-mile-long Lake Sunapee with its steamboat culture was a vacation destination for people from Boston and New York. Today, crowds of people make the journey into the center of Newport every Friday afternoon for live music, special events, and artist demonstrations. A story time for children is presented each week at 4pm by the Richards Free Library.

I stopped by on one summer afternoon to find spinning and woodworking demonstrations, lively music from a local folk band, and an impromptu petting zoo featuring a pair of handsome llamas. In addition to the array of activities, you will find more than forty vendors selling staples such as produce, meat, eggs, potted plants, cut flowers, baked goods, and prepared foods. Other interesting finds include elk sausage, zucchini relish, pickled green beans (also known as dilly beans), and good old-fashioned blueberry pie.

Peterborough Farmers' Market

Depot Square Park, Peterborough
Wednesday 3pm–6pm, May–October
www.peterboroughfarmersmarketnh.com

Peterborough is a town with rich cultural offerings, which include The MacDowell Colony for writers; the classical music venue, Monadnock Music; and the oldest operating summer theater in the country, the Peterborough Players, as well as art galleries, museums, fine dining options, and high-quality, locally owned shops. Thornton Wilder wrote *Our Town* while a resident at MacDowell, modeling the quintessential American community, Grover's Corners, after Peterborough.

The Peterborough Farmers' Market may be small, but given its location in the bustling Depot Square Park shopping area, it absolutely warrants a visit. The Park sits at the confluence of the Nubanusit and Contoocook rivers, which provide a soothing backdrop. Enjoy browsing the hearty selection of produce, tempting baked goods, and gorgeous bouquets of flowers.

Continue the local shopping experience at Depot Square. Spend some time at Bowerbird & Friends, which offers a beautifully curated selection of antique furniture, vintage finds, and handmade jewelry. In the back of the shop, a small greenhouse room is filled with topiaries and unusual plants. Also worth a stop is Red Chair Antiques, with its European flea market vibe, brimming with vintage buttons, linens, and other ephemera.

Hanover Farmers' Market

The Green, Hanover

Wednesday 3pm–6pm, June–September

www.hanoverchamber.org

Hanover, home to Dartmouth College, boasts a happening farmers' market scene. Although most of the student body packs up and heads home for the summer months, local residents and summer visitors fill The Green every Wednesday.

More than twenty local farms, as well as several artisan vendors, provide plentiful offerings. Members of the League of New Hampshire Craftsmen are often on hand giving demonstrations and selling their wares. Look for beautiful carved wooden spoons and toys, hand-dyed textiles, a variety of yarns and knitted goods, and handwoven baskets.

If you only make one stop at this market, it should be at the popular Vermont Crêpe and Waffle stand. Though there is often a long line, be sure not to miss their fresh-off-the-griddle treats. There's a savory, gluten-free buckwheat crêpe filled with Vermont cheeses, local eggs, caramelized onions, and sautéed spinach. Perhaps even more tempting is the dessert crêpe, which may be topped with chocolate sauce, seasonal berries, and whipped cream. . . or keep it plain with a drizzle of locally produced Vermont maple syrup.

Salmon Falls Mills Open Studios

The Mills at Salmon Falls, 1 Front Street, Rollinsford
Twice a year: Saturday before Mother's Day in May and
Saturday–Sunday before Thanksgiving, 10am–5pm
www.millartists.com

More than 100 artists occupy this renovated mill building in the small historic brick community of Rollinsford. For a century and a half, the Salmon Falls River, which divides New Hampshire from Maine, powered the textile mill here. In our time, two open houses a year draw hundreds of visitors to witness the studios workings of a wide variety of artists.

As you wander along the brick corridors of the beautifully restored building, look for David Random, who creates sculptures from salvaged mechanical parts. His ever-expanding collection of found and vintage spare parts lines an entire wall of pegboard in his space. In direct contrast to his metal-filled space is Jeanne Freeze's studio, where she works on projects for her company, Creek Hill Upholstery. The floor-to-ceiling shelves in the warm, intimate space are filled with trims, tassels, ribbons, and fabrics in every color. Similarly, the walls of fiber artist Tinka Pritchett's studio are covered

with richly colored fabric swatches; her large, inviting work space is filled with felting projects in various stages of completion. Every available nook and cranny in Stan Moeller's studio is hung with his oil paintings, with his easel and ongoing work taking center stage. A final favorite: Elizabeth Doherty's studio, dominated by the loom on which she weaves discarded plastic bags into beautiful, colorful, and functional pieces such as belts and handbags.

Squam Art Fair

Rockywold-Deephaven Camp, Holderness
Held twice a year, early June and mid-September,
Saturday 7:30pm–10pm
(check website for exact dates)
www.squamartworkshops.com

Squam Art Workshops (SAW) were founded in 2008 by Elizabeth MacCrellish as a gathering place for creative individuals to work with accomplished teachers. During these weekends, participants, guided by expert artists, can try their hand at almost any art form, including painting, knitting, photography, fiber arts, sewing, and mixed media. SAW takes place near the small town of Holderness which sits on Squam Lake.

On Saturday night of both the spring and fall retreats, workshop teachers and local shops offer their goods for sale at the Squam Art Fair, a rousing event open to the public. With nearly forty vendors, you will find everything from yarn, clothes, and vintage linens to art prints, books, and photographs. A party-like atmosphere pervades, complete with free beer, twinkling lights hung from the rafters, and raffle prizes galore. A crowd usually gathers before the doors open, eager to snap up handcrafted goods from their favorite vendors—be sure to get there on time for the best selection and remember: if you see something you love, buy it right then and there, as the one-of-a-kind goods on display here tend to go quickly.

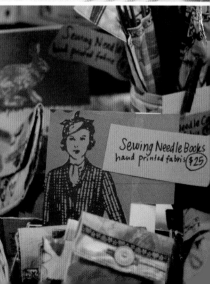

Sewing Needle Books
hand printed fabrics $25

League of NH Craftsmen's Fair

Mount Sunapee Resort, Newbury
Nine-day event, beginning on the first Saturday in August,
10am–5pm
www.nhcrafts.org

The first League of NH Craftsmen's Fair, held in 1933, was met with such enthusiasm that it was made an annual event. Although the event moved around the area for many years, it has now settled down at Mount Sunapee Resort, where it has been held since 1964. As the state's largest art festival, the fair features more than 200 booths and a packed schedule of live music, craft demonstrations, workshops, and performances by storytellers and theater groups.

Browsing the many booths can easily take an afternoon, so plan on arriving in the morning and devoting an entire day to the fair. Scattered among the booths are tents reserved for artist demonstrations by juried members of the League, ranging from papermaking to furniture building. Canterbury Shaker Village, the Granite State Woodcarvers, and more than twenty New Hampshire Craft Guilds and other groups committed to preserving traditional arts are also invited to demonstrate. Workshops for adults and children on a variety of topics—soap carving, glass blowing, basket weaving, and more—provide an opportunity to learn from master craftsmen. Some classes are free, but many require pre-registration and a fee. Check the website for a daily schedule; the small admission charge covers two days.

Oatmeal
Raisin
$ 2.25

Strawb...
Cheese Da...
$ 3.00

VERMONTER
Oats, Raisins,
FLAX, SUNFLOWER+
SESAME SEEDS
MAPLE SYRUP $ 2.25

Vermont

Farmers' Markets

Craft Markets

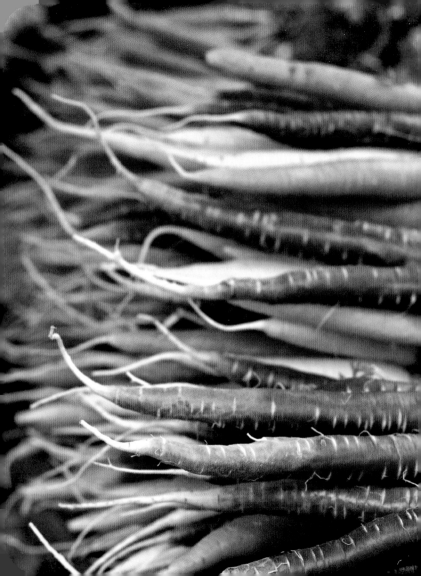

Burlington Farmers' Market

Summer: City Hall Park, Burlington
Saturday 8:30am–2pm, May–October

Winter: Memorial Auditorium, 250 Main Street, Burlington
Twice a month on Saturday, 10am–2pm

www.burlingtonfarmersmarket.org

Founded with just six vendors, the Burlington's Farmers' Market has grown over the past three decades and now welcomes over sixty farmers and food purveyors, as well as several artists, to City Hall Park every Saturday. Among the many nutritious prepared food options, you'll find hummus at Chick Peace; veggie crumble, a ground meat alternative, at Folk Foods; Triple Nut Butter made from almonds, cashews, and pecans at The Nutty Vermonter; and granola at Green Mountain Granola. A diverse range of ethnic prepared food offerings include Tibetan, Himalayan, Caribbean, and Thai cuisine. If your taste buds are craving something a bit closer to home, look no further than Stony Pond Farm's 100% organic, free-range beef burgers served with a thick slice of Vermont cheddar.

Waitsfield Farmers' Market

Mad River Green, Route 100, Waitsfield
Saturday 9am–1pm, May–October
www.waitsfieldfarmersmarket.com

It seems that most of the population of Mad River Valley turns out every Saturday to partake in the festivities at the Waitsfield Farmers' Market. Face painting, arts and crafts, live music, and a large picnic area all contribute to the country fair–like atmosphere.

More than sixty vendors offer their wares for sale; space is equally shared among agricultural, crafts, and prepared food booths. With so many vendors on hand, the specialty food items available are delightfully varied, including grass-fed yak meat from the Vermont Yak Company, freshly baked bagels from KC's Bagel Café, samosas from the Samosaman, dopyaza and vegetable mantu from Pakistani Foods, tamales from Grace's Tamales, and locally produced wines from East Shore Vineyard. Be on the lookout for Gizmo's Pickled Plus, with more than thirty kinds of organic pickles, jams, and chutneys, and Vermont Hills Teriyaki marinades, which come in original, double garlic, and sweet onion flavors.

Anyone who realizes how difficult it is to find locally and organically grown grains will be especially excited to find the Nitty Gritty Grain Company, selling cornbread, pancake, and muffin mixes, as well as soy beans, wheat berries, and unbleached all-purpose and pastry flour.

Brattleboro Farmers' Market

Wednesday 10am–2pm, Gibson-Aiken Center on Main Street
Saturday 9am–2pm, Route 9 just past the
Creamery Covered Bridge, June–October
www.brattleborofarmersmarket.com

In contrast to Brattleboro's bustling Saturday market, the town's Wednesday market, located in a shady, tree-lined alley off Main Street, offers a quiet, peaceful shopping experience. The selection is somewhat limited, but you can still find abundant produce, plenty of fresh-cut flowers, and a wide variety of baked goods. The highlight of the market is, without a doubt, the Thai food cart, which serves up an enticing menu of lunch items. Grab a plate of pad thai, chicken curry, or vegetable stir-fry, park yourself at one of the shady tables abutting the market, and savor the laid-back experience.

Brattleboro's large and lively Saturday market has a Sixties' back-to-the-land vibe and is held on an open grassy plot near the Creamery Covered Bridge. More than fifty vendors display their wares, which range from produce and prepared foods to pottery and knitted goods. A large sandbox provides the perfect distraction for the many children in attendance, and frees up parents to focus on shopping. Live music, ranging from bluegrass to jazz, fills the air as locals and visitors mix and mingle. There is a real sense of community here, largely due to the fact that many of the farms in the area are multi-generational and, over the years, strong bonds have formed between vendors and customers.

Lilac Ri

Middlebury Farmers' Market

Summer: By the Falls at the Marble Works, Middlebury
Wednesday 9am–12:30pm, June–October
Saturday 9am–12:30pm, May–October

Winter: American Flatbread at the Marble Works, Middlebury
Every Saturday 9:30am–1pm, November–December
2nd and 4th Saturday 9:30am–1pm, January–April

www.middleburyfarmersmarket.org

The Middlebury Farmers' Market is held in the park adjacent to the historic Marble Works section of Middlebury village, which overlooks the crashing Otter Creek Falls. More than sixty vendors turn out twice a week to sell fruit, vegetables, potted plants, flowers, dairy products, meat, and crafts, but the delectable prepared foods are what really steal the show.

Lucinda Rooney, a renowned artist and horticulturist who also dabbles in cooking, serves up an artfully displayed variety of sweet and savory treats, such as heirloom tomato quiche and rose petal cupcakes. Vergennes Laundry, a Vermont-based bakery, offers tempting delicacies such as pain au chocolat, plum almond puff, tomato melon tart, apple galette, and string bean fennel tart. If you are feeling adventurous, you might try the B.L.T. tart with Vermont smoked and cured bacon, locally sourced radish sprouts, baby arugula, Juliet tomatoes, and basil, all served in a flaky crust and drizzled with champagne vinaigrette. With prepared foods of this quality, the Middlebury Farmers' Market makes for the perfect lunchtime destination.

Queen City Craft Bazaar

Union Station, 1 Main Street, Burlington
Saturday 10am–5pm in early May and late November
www.queencitycraft.com

You would think a city as hip and youthful as Burlington would have an overflowing roster of indie art events, but until recently, there was no market, festival, or bazaar devoted to showcasing the many talented indie designers and artists of Vermont. Now, the Queen City Craft Bazaar has stepped in to fill the void. This juried show highlights more than forty of the best, most creative artists in the state.

Be prepared to find plenty of one-of-a-kind, funky offerings including cuff links from COOB Originals made out of reclaimed skateboards, colorful felted pillows by Woollymama, crocheted ice cream cones from urban-farmgirl, earrings made from zippers by Stacie Mincher, and jewelry from Subsixstudios. The quality and uniqueness of the products at the Queen City Craft Bazaar are among the best of the many craft shows I have attended The bazaar has recently added a holiday event in addition to the spring sale.

Vermont Crafts Council
Open Studio Weekend

Statewide (map on website)
Saturday–Sunday 10am–5pm, Memorial Day Weekend
www.vermontcrafts.com/links/open.html

More than 300 artists participate in the Vermont Crafts Council Open Studio Weekend, representing dozens of crafts. In addition to studio tours, many of the artists also give demonstrations throughout the weekend.

Because this event spans the entire state, the best way to plan an itinerary is to pick one county as a focus, and chart a route that includes the artists who have captured your attention. I picked Windham County in Southern Vermont and planned my weekend around visits to a wide variety of participants that include glassblowers, potters, painters, weavers, woodworkers, and jewelers. Many artists offer marked-down items and seconds.

A well-planned route might allow for five to seven studio visits a day, which leaves plenty of time for driving between locations and stopping along the way for coffee, snacks, and picturesque views that simply beg for a moment of your time. Many of the studios are tucked away down winding country roads, but as you near each studio, yellow signs mark the route, providing assurance that you are on the right track. If your route includes a major town, you might be able to catch one of the special exhibits or gallery talks held in conjunction with this event.

Vermont Festival of the Arts

Mad River Valley
Month of August (see website for calendar)
www.vermontartfest.com

This Festival was founded in 1997 to raise awareness of the rich community of artists and craftspeople who call Mad River Valley home. The goal was to provide both locals and visitors a chance to experience, explore, and participate in the making and viewing of art, from the visual and performance arts to the culinary and literary. The scope of activities over the course of a month includes open studio tours; cooking and art classes; theater performances; gallery exhibitions; a lecture series; and more.

The Festival kicks off with A Taste of the Valley at Sugarbush, in which local restaurants and food purveyors offer samples of their culinary specialties; live music, a silent auction, and wine and beer tastings round out the evening. A packed schedule runs through August, with several events a day. Highlights include The Big Flea, Open Studio Weekend, World Culinary Odyssey, The Valley Stage Music Festival, Yestermorrow Lecture Series, Big Red Barn Art Show, Innovative Homes of the Mad River Valley tour, Localvore Community Table Dinner, and various

theater and musical events held at The Big Picture Theater and Café. The Festival concludes with the Mad River Valley Craft Fair, held on Labor Day Weekend, with more than 100 juried vendors.

Many of the events are free and require no registration, but workshops, certain lectures, and many of the performances do require pre-registration and a fee. Check the Festival website for complete details. Be sure not to overlook the Artful Lodgers package, which offers visitors a discount on area hotels, inns, and bed-and-breakfasts.

The welcoming community of Mad River Valley helps to make this one-of-a-kind event a true celebration of the arts. Moments like one during the Art in the Garden tour—I found myself standing in the meticulously cultivated fields of Small Step farm, listening to the young, energetic owner describe the local food scene, while in the background, artist Joyce Kahn drew the farm in pastels—encapsulate the merging of community, local food, and art at the heart of the Vermont Festival of the Arts.

Vermont Sheep and Wool Festival

Tunbridge Fairgrounds, Tunbridge
Saturday 10am–5pm and Sunday 10am–4pm in early October
www.vermontsheep.org/festival.html

If you are enthralled with the idea of turning a simple ball of yarn into something both useful and beautiful—whether by sewing, knitting, or crocheting—you will be drawn to the Vermont Sheep and Wool Festival, which celebrates the fiber arts.

The weekend is filled with presentations, classes, and demonstrations on fiber skills (including spinning, felting, dyeing, and knitting) and animal husbandry (raising sheep, Border Collie herding, and shearing). The many varieties of sheep and goats on display definitely steal the show, as do the llamas, Angora rabbits, and alpacas.

The extensive marketplace is dedicated to fiber-related products such as felted jewelry, knitting supplies, handcrafted tools for spinners and weavers, rug hooking kits, and finished knitted items (sweaters, hats, scarves, baby booties). Among the natural and hand-dyed yarns and fibers for sale, you'll find wool, mohair, merino, and angora, as well as roving, and—for those interested in cleaning, dyeing and spinning their own yarn—raw fleece. Admission is $6.

Similar festivals are held in New Hampshire, Rhode Island, Connecticut, and Massachusetts; vermontsheep.org provides links to its New England counterparts.

Massachusetts

Farmers' Markets

Craft Markets

Boston Copley Square Farmers' Market

St. James Avenue, Dartmouth Street,
and Boylston Street, Boston
Tuesday and Friday 11am–6pm, May–November
www.massfarmersmarkets.org

Set in the heart of downtown Boston, the Copley Square Farmers' Market bustles with activity twice a week, and serves as a tempting lunchtime destination for food lovers who work in the area. With park benches galore, ample lawn space, and plenty of shady trees, Copley Square is an ideal picnicking location. Grab a brown bag picnic lunch from Crystal Brook Farm, or one of the many tempting sandwiches (poached chicken sandwich with bacon, avocado, caramelized onions, and herb aioli) from The Herb Lyceum at Gilson's. Top it off with sweets from The Danish Pastry House and a fresh lemonade and find yourself a comfortable spot to dig in.

What impressed me most about this market, besides being the perfect urban picnicking spot, was the sheer abundance of produce, much of it organic. Different heirloom varieties available were almost too numerous to count. Interesting finds included several types of mushrooms, black and red currants, squash blossoms, Persian cucumbers, and rainbow carrots.

Newton Farmers' Market at Cold Spring Park

Cold Spring Park, 1200 Beacon Street, Newton
Tuesday 1:30pm–6pm, July–October
www.massfarmersmarkets.org

Visit the Newton Farmers' Market in mid-summer, the ideal time to find a grassy spot and settle in with a bag of juicy plums, peaches, and nectarines. You'll find not only delicious in-season stone fruit from Noquochoke Orchards, but, in addition to a wide variety of other fruits and vegetables, an impressive offering of seventy different varieties of apples, including old favorites such as Golden Delicious and Cortland, as well as newer varieties such as Mutsu, Candy Crisp, Honeycrisp, and Jonagold. But even this profusion is only a small part of this market's cornucopia of delights.

Held at Cold Spring Park, this weekly afternoon market draws a large crowd, who also come for the baked goods, meats (including delicious turkey from Bob's Turkey Farm), seafood, potted and cut flowers, artisan cheeses, and homemade ice cream. Sheng Lor of Hmong Farms offers an expansive variety of Asian produce. Be on the lookout for hard-to-find herbs and greens such as sorrel, amaranth, bok choy, water spinach, and pea tendrils.

Our Own
Fresh Picked
Sweet
Onions
$ 3.50 /Bunc

Orleans Farmers' Market

21 Old Colony Way, Orleans, Cape Cod
Saturday 8am–12pm, May–November
www.orleansfarmersmarket.com

Freshly caught lobsters, sun-ripened peaches, just-picked corn, juicy heirloom tomatoes: no menu is better suited for summertime dining on Cape Cod, and there is no better local venue to find these ingredients than the Orleans Farmers' Market. In addition to summer staples, this small market offers such varied delicacies as gluten-free baked goods and native fruit vinaigrettes from The Optimal Kitchen, fresh quail eggs from Caroline's Corner, and smoked meats and fish from Dave's Ribs.

The variety of food items is matched by the impressive array of plants from Herring River Gardens, Bon Terra Nursery, and Sweetfern, which specialize in hundreds of hosta varieties. Gardeners will also delight in the worm products from Woo's Worms, including worm compost, live red wigglers, worm compost tea, and ready-for-use worm composting boxes.

The Orleans Farmers' Market also offers the perfect opportunity to find unique gifts, including beeswax candles from E & T Farms and flower arrangements and lavender sachets from Sea Turtle Farm; also look for colorfully packaged, handmade soaps from Summer House Natural Soaps.

West Tisbury Farmers' Market

Old Agricultural Hall (aka: Old Grange), 1067 State Road,
West Tisbury, Martha's Vineyard
Wednesday 9am–12pm, June–August
Saturday 9am–12pm, June–October
www.westtisburyfarmersmarket.com

If you are lucky enough to visit Martha's Vineyard during the summer months, you will notice an abundance of farm stands lining the island roads. While it is fun to spend the day bouncing from one stand to another, stocking up on cartons of berries, freshly baked pies, and organic vegetables, nothing beats the convenience of one-stop shopping. The West Tisbury Farmers' Market offers plenty of predictable market finds, as well as several unique, tasty offerings including artisan chocolates, sweet cream butter, fresh raspberry crushed ice, and the most diverse selection of heirloom tomatoes I have found. In addition to all the good eats, you will find alpaca yarn, succulent plantings, herbal body products, fragrant island-grown lavender sachets, and a host of other interesting artisan goods. All products are grown or made on the island. There is also a winter market held every second Saturday in October, November, and December at the Martha's Vineyard Agricultural Society at 35 Panhandle Road.

Sustainable Nantucket's Farmers and Artisans Market

North Union Street and Cambridge Street
Saturday 9am–1pm, June–October
www.sustainablenantucket.org

This market is sponsored by Sustainable Nantucket, whose mission—to "preserve the community character of Nantucket while sustaining its economic and environmental vitality"—is supported each week by this downtown event. It's a truly local affair, as all the vendors are required to be seasonal or year round residents of Nantucket, and all of the goods sold grown or produced on the island.

The market is equal parts fresh farm offerings and artisan wares. Pumpkin Pond Farm, Bartlett's Ocean View Farm, and Moors End Farm not only bring their produce and flowers to market each Saturday, but also open their farms for tours and shopping during the week. The variety of mushrooms available at Nantucket Mushrooms would make any foodie swoon; don't miss the tantalizing display of lovely pink, white, and golden oyster mushrooms.

The island's many artisans offer a host of handcrafted items including soap, quilts, knitted goods, tiles, ceramics, and wooden crafts. Standouts include the beeswax goods from Nantucket Honey Bee Co., as well as Seaweaver's luscious woven scarves, baby booties, and flower pins made from recycled sweaters.

SoWa Open Market

460 Harrison Avenue, Boston
Sunday 10am–4pm, May–October
www.sowaopenmarket.com

Mustache-shaped pillows, hipster T-shirts, vintage jewelry, kooky plush toys. . . these are just a few of the many funky wares you can expect to find at the SoWa Open Market (SoWa refers to its location South of Washington Street). A rotating group of 100 to 140 artists and designers keep things fresh—every Sunday offers an opportunity to find something new. A farmers' market and a vintage market are held in conjunction with the craft event, and you can spend an entire day hopping from one to the next. In addition to artists, be on the lookout for an eclectic mix of antique dealers, bakers, cheesemongers, and greengrocers, as well as a gourmet food truck court, which features a rotating group of eight to ten trucks.

Be sure not to miss the South End Open Studios weekend (Saturday–Sunday in late September), in which all of the major art buildings in the South End are open to the public, including the Boston Center for the Arts, Laconia Lofts, the SoWa buildings, studios on Wareham and Albany Streets, the Art Block, and the Piano Factory. All in all, more than 250 of Boston's artists open their studios to the public. In conjunction with the event, the SoWa Open Market invites more than 120 artists to participate in a special, two-day market. There is also a SoWa Holiday Market (www.sowaholidaymarket.com).

North River Arts Society Festival of the Arts

157 Old Main Street, Marshfield Hills
Saturday–Sunday 10am–5pm, Memorial Day Weekend
www.northriverarts.org

Although the North River Arts Society Festival of the Arts is one of the smaller art events featured in this book, the atmosphere is among the liveliest and most welcoming. The entire community of Marshfield Hills seems to be in attendance at this annual family-friendly event. Main Street is blocked off as artists' tents, activity stations, and food stands replace traffic. Plenty of enticing activities for kids include face painting, art projects, and games.

Many of the artists make time throughout the day to demonstrate their craft for the crowds. Judging from a crowd that gathered to see Mike McCarthy of Mattapoisett Bird Works hand-carve exquisite wooden birds, I'm not alone in my enthusiasm for the unique artist-attendee connection that this event seems to encourage.

Berkshires Art Festival

Ski Butternut, 380 State Road, Route 23, Great Barrington

Friday–Sunday of July 4th weekend

www.berkshiresartsfestival.com

The lodge staff at Ski Butternut might be accustomed to providing a refuge from the cold for weary downhill skiers, but every July, they shift gears, crank up the air conditioning, and welcome 175 artists and craftsmen for the annual Berkshires Art Festival. The lodge itself houses a handful of vendors, with the rest scattered over the base of Ski Butternut's scenic slopes. The idyllic setting is only part of this festival's charm.

Among the many routine wares, several artists with unique offerings stand out from the crowd. Adirondack Guide Boats, a renowned maker of wooden and Kevlar boats, offer exquisite vessels for sale. Marsya Jewelry's beautiful booth features handcrafted, yoga-inspired necklaces and bracelets. The Modern Dream, one of the only vendors with a youthful, indie feel, sells a wide variety of colorful felted bowls and trivets. Allen Design Studio specializes in organically shaped pottery bowls, cups, and vases.

Wandering the slopes, you will encounter artist demonstrations. Raku potter Richard Foye fires his ovens up to demonstrate the various glazing techniques that result from burning different fuels, including moose dung, pine shavings, straw, and pinecones. Also on hand is a crew from The Heartwood School for the Home-building Crafts demonstrating various timber framing techniques. Admission is $11.

Boston Bazaar Bizarre

Summer: Saturday in late August (see website for times)
Union Square, Somerville

Winter: Sunday in early December (see website for times)
The Cyclorama at the Boston Center for the Arts
539 Tremont Street, Boston

www.bazaarbizarre.org

The first Bazaar Bizarre, held in the Boston area in 2001, was organized by a small group of friends selling handcrafted goods. The grassroots concept quickly caught on, and soon Bazaar Bizarres were being held during the December holiday shopping season in Los Angeles, Cleveland, and San Francisco. Because of the great success of the holiday market, which boasts close to 100 vendors, the Boston Bazaar Bizarre now holds a summer event as well, with forty participating.

You will definitely not find reindeer sweaters or crocheted doilies here—as Bazaar Bizarre's slogan promises, this is "not your granny's craft fair." Instead, a hip, do-it-yourself energy surges through both the summer and winter fairs. Many of the wares tend more toward an indie, punk sensibility—you may come across messenger bags embroidered with skulls, T-shirts emblazoned with robots, and bowls made out of melted LP records—but if your taste is more subtle and sophisticated, there is still plenty for you. My favorites include Zoe Wyner's simple and elegant pottery, Olaria Studio's patterned ceramic jewelry, and Albertine Press's bold, ethnic-inspired stationery.

New Bedford Open Studios

New Bedford

First weekend in October, Saturday 10am–5pm and
Sunday 11am–5pm

www.newbedfordopenstudios.org

The College of Visual and Performing Arts at UMass Dartmouth opened its Star Store campus here in 2001 in a historic former department store. Many of the artists who study there have stayed in the city, and now this once-sleepy town has been transformed into a vibrant creative community. During Open Studio weekend, the public is invited to peek into the studios where many of the town's talented artists work.

Part of the appeal of the event is the opportunity to explore the historic structures that house many of them, including several beautifully renovated mill buildings and a former church. More than ninety artists open their work spaces for the weekend, but if there is one must-see destination, it is the Hatch Street Studios, located just north of downtown.

You can download a map online, grab one at any studio en route, or stop by the National Park Visitor Center, located at 33 William Street in downtown New Bedford, for more information. Since numerous studios are housed at each site, and the destinations are all close to each other, you can easily cover all the locations over the course of the weekend.

Twist

Northampton Center for the Arts
17 New South Street, Northampton
Friday–Saturday, twice a year in May and November
www.twistfair.com

Twist features more than sixty vendors selling everything from knitwear and apparel to metalwork and ceramics. The fair kicks off on Friday evening with the Market Party, a rousing event that helps set this craft fair apart from the others. At the party, enjoy a first look at all the goods while enjoying tastings of local beers and the DJ. The party-like atmosphere definitely puts visitors in the mood for shopping; if you see something that catches your eye, don't hesitate to claim it right away as your own.

The event continues throughout the day on Saturday, though things are a bit more toned down than at the previous night's affair. I'm always excited to see the newest offerings from many of my favorite Massachusetts-based artists, including Sarah Ahearn's mixed-media pieces, Beehive Kitchenware's whimsical kitchen goods, Happy Owl Glassworks' fused glass cuff links, Pressbound's wood-block stationery, and wacky stuffed animals by Zooguu. Admission is $4.

Rhode Island

Farmers' Markets

Craft Markets

Southside Community Land Trust Annual Rare and Unusual Plant Sale

City Farm, Corner of Dudley Street and
West Clifford Street, Providence

Saturday–Sunday, 10am–2pm the weekend after Mother's Day

www.southsideclt.org/plantsale

The mission of the three-decade-old Southside Community Land Trust has been to build community through urban agriculture. This thriving sense of green-thumb camaraderie is exactly what makes its annual plant sale, held at the SCLT City Farm location in South Providence, a not-to-be-missed event. Although all the usual vegetables and herbs—including salad greens, basil, rosemary, lavender, and several unique varieties of mint and tomatoes—are available, the rare and exotic plants tend to elicit the most excitement. You will find hundreds of varieties of vegetable and fruit seedlings, as well as annuals, perennials, and culinary and medicinal herbs. Several gardening experts are on hand to answer questions.

With live music, an ice cream truck, and a turnout usually close to 2,000, this event is a festive kickoff to the growing season. All proceeds from the plant sale support SCLT's educational and community gardening programs.

fresh YOGURT

Kefir

PRICES

fresh MOZZARELLA	$5 / BALL
SMOKED MOZZARELLA	$6 / BALL
Ricotta 1 lb tub $5.00	Ricotta 1½ Tin $6.30
Kefir Bottle $2.00 Kefir cup $3.00	Yogurt $2.80 ⅔ tub * BUY 4 GET ONE FREE
ANGELITO plain or herb + garlic or Jalapeño	$5.50
Pirate Spread sun-dried tomatoes, rosemary, feta base $5.75 $4	OLIVE TREASURE $5.75
GOAT CHEESE	Queso Fresco 6.50

SALE

RICotta Ricotta

$2 off am $76

Narragansett Creamery

www.richeese.com

Hope Street Farmers' Market

Lippitt Park (Hope Street and Blackstone Boulevard.), Providence
Saturday 9:30am–12:30pm, June–October
www.farmfreshri.org

My ideal Saturday morning includes a leisurely walk to the local farmers' market, which, for me, is the bustling Hope Street Farmers' Market. Here, I can get all of my weekly grocery shopping done, from bread, cheese, yogurt, and meats to fruit, vegetables, and fresh flowers. Although I would love to see a wider variety of specialty and heirloom produce, I can always count on this market to stock the staples.

I always begin my shopping with a quick walk-through to view all the offerings. Since shopping always seems more pleasant with refreshments in hand, I usually start with a pastry from Seven Stars Bakery and a coffee from New Harvest Coffee Roasters. During the steamy summer months, I simply can't resist sampling the many unique flavors from Rhode ILin Ice Cream, a local, artisanal ice cream vendor. No matter how full I might be at this point, I still manage to sneak in a few samples of cheese from Farmstead and Narragansett Creamery.

Notwithstanding all the tasty treats, the atmosphere of the market is perhaps its greatest appeal. The East Side of Providence has a very family-friendly vibe, which is echoed at the Hope Street market. Every week there is musical entertainment aimed at the younger crowd, and while the kids dance to their hearts' delight, parents often grab a seat on the grass and indulge in spontaneous picnicking.

Southside Community Land Trust

City Farm

City sown. City grown.

SEVEN STARS BAKERY ★

Coastal Growers' Market

Summer: Casey Farm, 2325 Boston Neck Road, Saunderstown
Saturday 9am–12pm, May–October

Winter: Lafayette Mill on Route 102, North Kingstown
Saturday 10am–1pm, November–April

www.coastalmarket.org

This organic farm, owned by Historic New England, boasts sweeping views of Narragansett Bay—its free-range cows and pigs reside on some of the best real estate in Rhode Island. A dedicated farm staff tends its fields and sells the bounty at these markets; dozens of other vendors also participate. During the week Casey Farm bustles with visiting school groups, who come to learn about life on a sustainable farm, but when Saturday rolls around, the real crowds descend.

The Coastal Growers' Market is a Class A market, which means that individual vendors can only sell what they themselves produce. In addition to plentiful fruit and vegetable offerings, be on the lookout for lobster and fresh seafood from Spencer Fish and Lobster, pasture-raised and grass-fed meats from Pat's Pastured, oysters from Matunuck Oyster Farm, homemade pasta sauces and salsa from Poblano Farms, fresh-from-the-oven pizza from Bravo Wood Fired Pizza, homemade pesto from Besto Pesto, and baked goods from Seven Stars Bakery and Olga's Cup and Saucer.

One advantage of a market held on a working farm is the chance to take a farm tour. On select Saturdays, other activities may include yoga on the lawn, old-fashioned kids' games, and live music.

Matunuck Oyster Farm

Matunuck Oysters	$10/doz
Little Necks	$5/doz
Mussels	$4/lb
Steamers	$4/lb
Lobsters	$8/lb

Aquidneck Growers' Market

Newport Vineyards & Winery, 909 East Main Road, Middletown

Saturday 9am–1pm, June–October

www.aquidneckgrowersmarket.org

Given its location on the picturesque grounds of Newport Vineyards, it would be easy for the scenery to steal the show at the Aquidneck Growers' Market, but thanks to a committed group of vendors, the market more than holds its own. Look for Rhode Island market staples from purveyors such as Custom House Coffee, Narragansett Creamery, Olga's Cup and Saucer, Farmstead Cheese, and Pat's Pastured. This is the only place where products from Aquidneck Honey and Aquidneck Farms are sold.

In what can only be described as a case of perfect timing, the market ends at 1pm, just when the first public tour of Newport Vineyard and Winery gets underway. It's worth sticking around, if for nothing else than a taste of the award-winning Riesling and White Vinifera Blend. To round out your local shopping experience, ask the winery staff to suggest a wine to accompany whatever farm-fresh meals you might have planned for the coming week—the winery's Vidal Ice Wine and a fresh peach cobbler are one such perfect pairing.

Pawtucket Wintertime Farmers' Market

Hope Artiste Village, 1005 Main Street, Pawtucket
Saturday 10am–1pm, Wednesday 4pm–7pm, November–May
www.farmfreshri.org

It used to be that the approach of colder weather meant the end of market season. Now, due to the increasing, year-round demand for local, sustainably produced food, this is no longer the case—winter markets are quickly gaining in popularity throughout New England. There is no better example of this trend than the bustling Pawtucket Wintertime Farmers' Market, located at the Hope Artiste Village, one of the largest mill restoration projects in Rhode Island. During the week, many artists and small businesses call this restored mill building their home, but on Wednesday evenings and Saturday mornings, the exposed brick hallways fill to the brim with locavores.

Although the array of produce is more limited in winter than summer, you can nevertheless expect to find a wide range of greens, root vegetables, apples, eggs, meat, breads, milk, pastries, oats, and cheeses. A rotating selection of prepared foods, from grilled cheese and Jamaican specialties, to organic salads and hot dogs, will satisfy your immediate hunger.

Really Good Vanilla
Bittersweet Chocolate
Organic Coffee
Olive Oil
Balsamic Vinegar
Local Blueber...

Zephyr Farm
Fresh Eggs
$5.00

Farm Fresh Rhode Island
Local Food Fest

Castle Hill Inn & Resort, 590 Ocean Drive, Newport
Weeknight in early August
www.farmfreshri.org

At the Local Food Fest, two dozen farmers team up with chefs from top Rhode Island restaurants to prepare tastings based on seasonal local ingredients. Held on the stunning oceanfront grounds of the Castle Hill Inn & Resort, the annual event benefits Farm Fresh Rhode Island, the organization responsible for supporting the local food movement. The evening celebrates the tiny state's farmers, food artisans, fishermen, and winemakers. The price of admission includes unlimited food samplings, as well as tastings of local wines and beers. Past delicacies have included pan-roasted striped bass with peaches, lamb sausage with purple potatoes and arugula, poached egg crostini, and blueberry ice cream with white and yellow peaches. Tickets are $45 (children under 12 free). I recommend that you purchase tickets in advance through the website; this event often sells out.

Please Try
One!!!
(or 2 or 3)

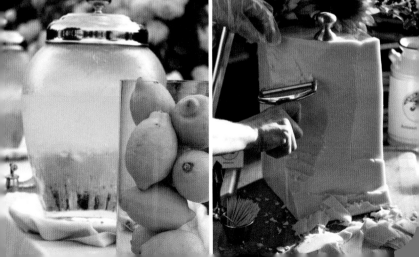

Providence Art Festival

Westminster Street and Eddy Street, Providence
Saturday in early June, 10:30am–6pm
www.indowncity.com/news

Downtown Providence has been revitalized in the past decade, with new shops and restaurants filling the once-vacant storefronts. No street has been transformed quite as drastically as Westminster Street, which has become a hip shopping and dining destination, as well as home to a variety of festivals and activities throughout the year. One such event is the Providence Art Festival, which stretches the length of the street and offers shoppers fabulous, funky art finds, great food, on-tap drinks, and live entertainment.

True to the city's nickname "The Creative Capital"—Providence is home to the Rhode Island School of Design—the goods found at this art festival are top notch. Jeweler Amie Plante sells rings, necklaces, and earrings, each an intricate stand-alone work of art. Zoetropa, a stationery line, sells playful office accessories perfect for jazzing up your cubicle. For youngsters, look for softies made from upcycled sweaters by Millie & Hazel Designs and high-quality, handmade wooden toys by Bearded Seal Woodcrafts.

Make an afternoon of it by browsing the shops on Westminster Street. A few of my favorites include Craftland, something of a permanent craft fair; Eno, a luxury wine store; Heir Antiques, a store that is always right on trend; and Symposium Books, an independent bookstore with a great selection of titles.

Indie Art by the Sea

Fort Adams State Park, Newport
Saturday in early July, 11am–5pm
www.indieartbythesea.com

As if Newport—with its pristine beaches, bustling shopping district, and legendary mansions—didn't boast enough charm to entice visitors during the summer months, there is now one more reason to visit. Set against the backdrop of Narragansett Bay and the Newport Harbor, Indie Art by the Sea offers craft enthusiasts a chance to browse the booths of more than 100 curated local and national artists who provide a wide range of unique, handmade items.

The vibe here tends more towards the indie arts, with hip, offbeat goods such as masking tape sculptures from Sarah Anne DiNarto, handprinted textiles from Redwing Hill, and pop-bottle jewelry from Wilton Artisans. This is an especially good market for children's products, with plenty of clever onesies, stuffed animals, accessories, and artwork for the little ones in your life, including stuffed gnomes from Fruit Cake Designs and hooded baby towels from Tess & Tallulah.

South Coast Artists Open Studio Tour

Tiverton and Little Compton, RI; Dartmouth and Westport, MA
(complete map on website)
Saturday–Sunday in mid-July and late-August, 11am–5pm
www.southcoastartists.org

The chance to poke around artists' studios is an invitation I can't resist, especially if those studios happen to be located along the breathtakingly gorgeous shores of coastal Rhode Island and Massachusetts.

The South Coast Artists Open Studio Tour encompasses over forty-five artist studios in four coastal towns—Westport and Dartmouth, Massachusetts, and Tiverton and Little Compton, Rhode Island. The self-guided tour will take you across farmland, down small coastal highways, and through quaint towns. During the drive, you will discover talented artists tucked away in welcoming studio spaces, working in a wide variety of mediums including watercolor, sculpture, ceramics, fiber arts, jewelry, wood, metal, acrylics, and oil.

Detailed maps are available online and at each site. Once you are on your way, look for the blue-and-white Open Studio signs and windsocks marking each gallery or studio on the tour. The destinations are relatively close together, so it is possible to cover a dozen or so stops per day. Take time to explore the coastal towns along the route.

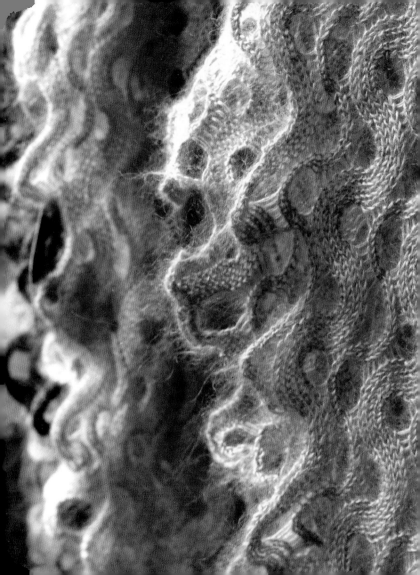

RISD Alumni and Student Art Sale

Benefit Street, Providence
Spring Sale held in early May
Fall Sale held in early October

Rhode Island Convention Center, One Sabin Street, Providence
Holiday Sale held in early December
Admission: $7

www.risd.edu

The annual Alumni and Student Art Sale of the renowned Rhode Island School of Design consistently draws large crowds, eager to snap up original works from both well-established and up-and-coming artists and designers. The spring and fall sales take place on Benefit Street, on a two-block stretch in front of the RISD Museum, while the holiday sale is held indoors at the Rhode Island Convention Center. More than 100 artists participate in this event, which is highly regarded among design cognoscenti. Vendors are chosen by lottery, so the roster changes quite a bit from event to event.

The items for sale include paintings, jewelry, clothing, home accessories, prints, furniture, and photography. Look for Anne Emlein Knitwear's gorgeous, geometric knit scarves, Elyse Allen Textiles' funky fingerless merino gloves, and Sovereign Beck's stylish neckties.

Connecticut

Farmers' Markets

Craft Markets

City Farmers' Market, Wooster Square

Russo Park, corner of Chapel Street and DePalma Court,
New Haven
Summer Market: Saturday 9am–1pm, May–December
Winter Market: Select Saturdays 10am–1pm, January–April
www.cityseed.org

The college town of New Haven, home to Yale University, has an enviable local food scene, with farmers' markets occurring almost daily throughout the city. At Saturday's Wooster Square market, you can look forward to scoring such hard-to-find delicacies as goat meat, tomato chutney, sheep's ricotta cheesecake, Cornish cross chickens, raw milk, and baked stuffed lobster tails. The crowd here is always lively—and hungry—so get to the market early for the best selection. Sankow's Beaver Brook Farm has prepared foods for those who prefer to spend their summer days on the beach instead of in the kitchen. Try the lamb Bolognese sauce or white bean chili for a quick, healthy, locally made meal.

Once you have finished up your shopping, stop by The Cheese Truck, which serves artisanal grilled cheese sandwiches with tasty add-ons such as guacamole and applewood bacon.

Coventry Regional Farmers' Market

Summer: Nathan Hale Homestead, 2299 South Street, Coventry
Sunday 11am–2pm, June–October

Winter: Sunday 11am–2pm, late November–February
Coventry High School, 78 Ripley Hill Road, Coventry

www.coventryfarmersmarket.com

Equal parts country fair and farmers' market, The Coventry Regional Farmers' Market feels like a momentous celebration each and every Sunday. Many dedicated shoppers arrive early to score a close parking spot, and to scope out the goods before the crowds descend. In fact, to discourage early birds, purchasing is not allowed to start until the bell rings at 11am on the dot.

You will find an enticing variety of organic and heirloom fruits and vegetables, grass-fed beef, smoked bacon, homemade pesto, spices and salsas, freshly baked breads and sweets, artisanal cheeses, and cut and potted flowers. Perhaps the most tempting treat of all is Farm to Hearth's wood-grilled pizzas, which are made to order with a wide variety of toppings. The market also features the work of local artists whose wares might include handcrafted soaps and beauty products, beeswax candles, hemp clothing, and hand-spun yarns.

Adding to the festive feel are the special events that take place week to week including the Heirloom Tomato Festival in late August; the Green Up, Connecticut event in early September; and the Harvest Pickin' and Bluegrass Jam in late October.

Stonington Farmers' Market

Town Dock at 4 High Street, Stonington

Saturday 9am–12pm, May–November

www.sviastonington.org/what.htm

The Stonington Farmers' Market is as picturesque as the seaside town itself. While it's chock full of farm-fresh edibles—fruit, vegetables, baked goods, dairy products, and meats—the real treat here is the vast array of seafood, much of it caught that morning. Stonington is home to the last commercial fishing fleet in the state of Connecticut, an ideal place to purchase fresh seafood.

Be on the lookout for scallops, clams, oysters, lobsters, and a wide variety of fish. If you need suggestions for how to prepare your fresh catch, ask any of the fishermen, who will share their favorite recipes which often incorporate other market items. Is it tomato season? Why not try the recipe for Tangy Tomato-Garlic Fish? Is corn at its sweetest? Try your hand at corn chowder with fresh clams. Once your shopping is complete, stroll along Stonington's charming quintessentially New England Main Street for a peek into the sweet local shops.

e Museum Outdoor Crafts Festival

1 Museum Drive, Greenwich
Saturday–Sunday in late May, one week before Memorial Day,
10am–5pm
www.brucemuseum.org

The Bruce Museum's beautiful grounds serve as the perfect backdrop for the annual Outdoor Crafts Festival. Drawing talented craftsmen and women from across the country, this festival highlights a wide range of artisanal goods, including jewelry, woodwork, fiber arts, furniture, and metalwork. While you will find many craft show staples similar to what is seen at many festivals, a handful of unique artists elevate this event from the ordinary.

Primitive Twig is a line of playful, colorful sculptures made from found and vintage items, such as antique doll parts, tins, scrap metal, and deconstructed old toys; the booth is clearly a show favorite. You'll find a crowd, too, at `e ko logic, where racks display fashionable skirts, tops, hats, and mittens fashioned from recycled post-consumer clothing, including cashmere.

The Bruce Museum's Outdoor Arts Festival, held annually on Columbus Day Weekend, features fine art including painting, graphics and drawing, mixed media, sculpture, and photography, unlike the Crafts Festival, which features more functional crafts. The $8 admission to either includes admission to the museum.

City-Wide Open Studios Weekend

New Haven

Three consecutive weekends, late September–early October

www.cwos.org

City-Wide Open Studios (CWOS) spans three weekends in the fall, with a jam-packed schedule that invites you to explore New Haven's diverse neighborhoods while discovering artist studios, alternative gallery spaces, and exhibitions.

This annual event begins with a kickoff party and gallery viewing featuring the work of CWOS participants at Artspace, the not-for-profit organizer. Different spaces are open each year —during the first weekend, Erector Square studios may be open to the public (Erector Square, a converted industrial warehouse that originally housed the factory for making Erector Toys). During the second weekend, visitors tour over 100 private artists' studios throughout New Haven. Ditch the car and bike from studio to studio along with the gang from Devil's Gear, the city's oldest and largest bike shop. During the third and final weekend, more than forty artists display their work in a gallery space.

The logistics of this event can be a bit confusing, so start your journey at Artspace, located at 50 Orange Street, which serves as the CWOS festival hub. Staff and volunteers are on hand throughout the event to answer any questions, and provide maps and detailed information. The schedule, locations, and range of events is subject to change year to year, so check the CWOS website for maps, schedules, and the most up-to-date information.

Roseland Cottage Fine Arts and Crafts Festival

556 Route 169, Woodstock
Saturday–Sunday following Columbus Day Weekend,
10am–4:30pm
www.historicnewengland.org

The Roseland Cottage Fine Arts and Crafts Festival, a two-day juried event featuring 175 artisans and their wares, is held on the grounds of the beautifully preserved and maintained Roseland Cottage. Artists display their goods, including jewelry, photographs, pottery, glass, paintings, and metalwork in booths lining the Cottage's exquisite Victorian gardens.

You can easily spend a day visiting Roseland Cottage. The property, owned by Historic New England, was built in 1846 in the Gothic Revival style. The grounds include an ice house, aviary, carriage barn, and indoor bowling alley. The residence's elaborately decorated first-floor rooms remain open during the festival for tours. The Columbus Day weekend falls at the perfect time of year to explore the country roads around Woodstock and indulge in leaf peeping, apple and pumpkin picking, and vineyard tours. Admission is $5.

Featured Artisans

Additional Resources

If you are interested in finding out more about shopping locally, please check out the many resources available nationally, regionally and by state.

National

Edible Communities · www.ediblecommunities.com

Indie Craft Shows · www.indiecraftshows.com

Local Harvest · www.localharvest.org

The 3/50 Project · www.the350project.net

New England

Seacoast Eat Local · www.seacoasteatlocal.org

Visit New England · www.visistnewengland.com

Maine

Maine Federation of Farmers' Markets · www.mffm.org

Maine Food and Lifestyle Magazine ·
www.mainefoodandlifestyle.com

Maine Organic Farmers and Gardeners Association ·
www.mofga.org

Maine. The magazine. · www.themainemag.com

New Hampshire

Edible White Mountains · www.ediblewhitemountains.com

New Hampshire Farmers' Market Association · www.nhfma.org

Vermont

Vermont Agency of Agriculture, Food and Markets ·
www.vermontagriculture.com

Massachusetts

Edible Boston · www.edibleboston.com

Edible Cape Cod · www.ediblecapecod.com

Edible Pioneer Valley · www.ediblepioneervalley.com

Edible South Shore · www.ediblesouthshore.com

Edible Vineyard · www.ediblevineyard.com

Federation of Massachusetts Farmer's Markets ·
www.massfarmersmarkets.org

Rhode Island

Edible Rhody · www.ediblerhody.com

Farm Fresh Rhode Island · www.farmfreshri.org

Visit Rhode Island · www.visitrhodeisland.com

Connecticut

Buy Connecticut Grown · www.buyctgrown.com

Connecticut Farm Fresh · www.ctfarmfresh.org

Edible Nutmeg · www.ediblenutmeg.com

Index

About the Author

Christine Chitnis is a writer, photographer, and environmental educator. She lives with her husband and son in Providence, Rhode Island. Her writing has appeared in *Country Living*, *Time Out New York*, *ReadyMade*, *Edible Rhody*, and *The Washington Post*, among many other local and national publications. She holds a degree in Environmental Science from the University of Colorado. Visit her at christinechitnis.com.

Photograph by Thea Coughlin

Experience a quintessentially American summer—a village-green, homemade-ice-cream, corn-on-the-cob kind of summer—exploring the fifty vibrant farmers' and artisan markets profiled in *Markets of New England*. You'll find picture-postcard settings, delicious food, and unique crafts down every ribbon of highway. Make your way up the coast to Cape Cod, where markets feature baskets of blueberries and flats of oysters still dripping with saltwater; hop the ferry to Sustainable Nantucket's picturesque farm stands; or journey inland to an art festival nestled in the Berkshires. In New Hampshire, attend a lakeside workshop and a market held on New England's largest town commons; in Vermont, an open studio weekend; in Maine, a clam festival, a county fair, and craft guild shows. Even tiny Rhode Island has pleasures aplenty: an ocean-front gourmet food tasting, an indie art fair overlooking Narragansett Bay and Newport Harbor, and more. *Markets of New England* leads you to the local delicacies, the most interesting purveyors, standout crafts and art, and provides all the details you need to know. The food and crafts are filled with local flavor, the settings pure New England, and the itineraries provide enough delights to fill an endless summer.

us $15.95 | $17.95 can | £9.99 uk

ISBN 978-1-892145-96-3

51595

Cover Design By: Lauren Ruggeri

The Little Bookroom
New York

www.littlebookroom.com